ROBERT SCHUMANN

FANTASIESTÜCKE

Violoncello and Piano / Violoncello und Klavier

op. 73

EIGENTUM DES VERLEGERS · ALLE RECHTE VORBEHALTEN
ALL RIGHTS RESERVED

EDITION PETERS

London · Frankfurt/M. · Leipzig · New York

Fantasie-Stücke

für
Klavier und Klarinette oder Violine

I

R. Schumann, Op. 73
Für Violoncello bearbeitet von
Friedrich Grützmacher

3

II

ROBERT SCHUMANN

FANTASIESTÜCKE

Violoncello and Piano / Violoncello und Klavier

op. 73

Violoncello

EIGENTUM DES VERLEGERS · ALLE RECHTE VORBEHALTEN
ALL RIGHTS RESERVED

EDITION PETERS

LONDON · FRANKFURT/M. · LEIPZIG · NEW YORK

Violoncello

II

Violoncello

III

Violoncello

Violoncello

III